Royal Arch, Capitular and Cryptic Masonry

By William F. Kuhn, William Potts George, Hugh McCurdy and Arthur Edward Waite

Copyright © 2019 Lamp of Trismegistus. All rights reserved. No part of this publication may be reproduced or transmitted in any form or by any means, electronic or mechanical, including photocopying, recording, or by any information storage and retrieval system, without permission in writing from Lamp of Trismegistus. Reviewers may quote brief passages.

ISBN: 978-1-63118-425-3

*Foundations of Freemasonry
Series*

Other Books in this Series and Related Titles

Masonic Symbolism of the Apron & the Altar by Albert G. Mackey, William Harvey, H. L. Haywood, Joseph Fort Newton and H. A. Kingsbury (978-1-63118-428-4)

Ancient Mysteries and Secret Societies by Manly P. Hall (978-1-63118-410-9)

Ancient Egyptian Mysteries and Hieroglyphics, Modern Freemasonry & Initiation of the Pyramid by Henry Ridgely Evans, Manly P. Hall, George Smith and Albert G. Mackey (978-1-63118-430-7)

The Lost Keys of Freemasonry or The Secret of Hiram Abiff by Manly P. Hall (978-1-63118-427-7)

The Book of Parables by Enoch (978-1-63118-429-1)

Symbolism of the Corner Stone, the North East Corner and the Religious & Masonic Symbolism of Stones by Albert G. Mackey, William Harvey and William Wynn Westcott (978-1-63118-412-3)

Rosicrucian and Masonic Origins by Manly P. Hall (978-1-63118-000-2)

The Philosophy of Masonry in Five Parts by Roscoe Pound (978-1-63118-004-0)

The Story and Legend of Hiram Abiff by William Harvey, Manly P. Hall and Albert G. Mackey (978-1-63118-411-6)

Symbolism and Discourses on the Entered Apprentice, Fellowcraft and Master Mason Blue Lodge Degrees by H. L. Haywood, Asahel W. Gage, William Harvey, Albert G. Mackey and Arthur Edward Waite (978-1-63118-413-0)

Audio Versions are also Available on Audible and iTunes

Table of Contents

Introduction...7

The York Rite
by William F. Kuhn...9

Masonic Tradition and the Royal Arch
by Arthur Edward Waite...15

High Purpose and Genius of Royal Arch Masonry
by William F. Kuhn...31

The Fourth Degree
by William F. Kuhn...47

Capitular Masonry
by William Potts George...57

The Birth of Cryptic Masonry
by Hugh McCurdy...71

Introduction

From the beginning of Modern Freemasonry's birthdate of 1717, the intelligentsia of humanity have found refuge for safe reflection within the walls of the fraternity. Masonic writers have produced a nearly incalculable amount of written musings on a multitude of esoteric and philosophical subjects, as they relate to the ancient mysteries that Freemasonry currently storehouses. Sadly, most of it appears to have sat largely unread, as American Freemasonry in particular, continues to transform itself into something that bears little resemblance to what it was originally designed to be. The true essence of Freemasonry is not that of blind patriotism or a single-minded national religion but one of Universal Brotherhood and altruism, designed for the betterment not just of its members but of society as a whole. In particular, for those who are not members of the fraternity, as Freemasonry has always acted as a beacon, to help guide humanity through darker times, with the hopes that one day we will collectively reach a truly enlightened age.

It's not uncommon for new members joining the fraternity to find little education within the walls of many modern lodges, in spite of so much written material available to the membership. Many older members are not simply uneducated with regards to real Masonic history and symbology, not to mention the vast arena of related subjects, but they are disinterested in all of it, as well.

Lamp of Trismegistus is doing its part to help preserve humanity's Masonic history by making some of these classics available to those students who are seeking to unearth the knowledge of these ancient colossi. As such, Lamp of Trismegistus offers its readers highlights of Masonic study, culled from a variety of authors and viewpoints, with the hope bringing education back into the fraternity. So, be sure to check out other titles in our *Foundations of Freemasonry Series* as well as our *Esoteric Classics, Theosophical Classics, Occult Fiction* and our *Christian Apocrypha Series,* and don't be afraid to let a little altruism into your own heart or even into your Lodge. You can also download the audio versions of most of these titles from iTunes or Audible.

The York Rite

By William F. Kuhn

It has been stated that "*A Rite in Freemasonry is a collection of grades or degrees always founded on the First three degrees.*" This definition is wholly misleading, and constitutes as grave an error as to call "The York Rite" as conferred in the United States, "The American Rite."

For the purpose of adding "more light" on the subject, we may state that in the United States there are two Masonic Rites, known as the York Rite and the Ancient and Accepted Scottish Rite.

Both are misnomers if the name of the Rite is to indicate its parentage or birthplace. The York Rite was not born in the ancient city of York, neither was the Ancient and Accepted Scottish Rite begotten in Scotland.

The so-called York Rite is the result of an evolution in England from a One Degree Operative Craft of 1717, to a system of degrees of six or more as now practiced in the United States, Canada, England, Scotland and Ireland. The Scottish Rite was evolved from the Rite of perfection of twenty-five Degrees, by the addition of eight more at Charleston, South Carolina, in 1801, where the Mother Supreme Council was formed.

If either one of the Rites is to be known as the American Rite, the title probably belongs to the Ancient and Accepted

Scottish Rite. To designate the so-called York Rite in the United States, as the American Rite, would be even more absurd than to call it the *York* Rite, for it is neither.

What is meant by the word Rite? A Rite is defined as "A custom of practice of a formal kind; a formal procedure of a religious or solemn observance." But such a religious or solemn procedure or observance must have a definite end or purpose. It must have a goal idea. A central idea, which the ceremony of procedure is intended to convey. The ceremony may be brief or voluminous, plain or ornate, but the central idea must be maintained and attained, as in the Rite of Baptism, in the Rite of Marriage, in the Rite of the Holy Sacrament, etc.

The central idea or pivot around which all Masonic ceremonies or Degrees must revolve is the Loss, the Recovery, and the Interpretation of the Master's word. This goal idea must be the nucleus of a system of Degrees, and without which no system of Degrees can be called a Rite.

Any series of Degrees, however intimately connected, that does not contain this central idea of Loss, Recovery, and interpretation can not be called a Masonic Rite. This is the goal idea or pivot of the so- called York Rite. The number of Degrees in a Rite is merely incidental. It matters not whether there are three or thirty-three Degrees, provided the central idea, the end of all Masonic symbolism is present.

The Loss and Recovery with a positive interpretation, or the Loss and Recovery with a general or individual interpretation is the very essence of a Rite.

The Loss is symbolized in the Craft or Lodge Degrees, the Recovery is symbolized in the Royal Arch.

In the York Rite the interpretation of the symbolism of the Royal Arch is left to the individual interpretation of the Royal Arch Mason, or it finds its positive and special interpretation in the light of the new dispensation, as taught in the Masonic Order of the Christian Knighthood.

The Three Craft or Blue Lodge Degrees, the Royal Arch, and the United Orders of the Temple and of Malta are the essential grades of the York Rite. The Mark, Past, Most Excellent, Royal, Select Degrees, and the Illustrious Order of the Red Cross are not essential, nor essentially necessary to the York Rite, but they are great aids in the elucidation of the symbolism of the central idea of the Rite and they adorn and magnify the Rite. The Lodge Degrees, the Royal Arch, and the Masonic Orders of Christian Knighthood constitute the so-called "York Rite." To eliminate the Royal Arch would be like removing the keystone of an arch, and the whole fabric would crumble and fall.

In essentials, the York Rite is the same in the United States as it is in every province or Country in the British Empire; in other words, it is essentially the same in the Anglo-Saxon world. But each country has its own system. In the United States it consists of seven Degrees and three Orders; in Canada, of six Degrees and three Orders, although Canada has added the most excellent Degree in the Chapter and the Red Cross of the Commandery to harmonize, for the purpose of visitation with the United States; in England, it consists of four

Degrees and two Orders; in Ireland, of five Degrees and two Orders; in Scotland the system conforms closely to that of Ireland. The most excellent Degree is unknown in the British Empire, except in Canada; in England, the Mark Master's Degree is under the control of a Grand Lodge of Mark Master Masons.

It will be noted that in the countries mentioned, the number of Degrees in the Rite varies, even the Degrees bearing the same name vary in the ceremonies of presenting the same truth. The Master's Degree in Pennsylvania varies much from the same Degree in the other States, yet symbolically it is the same. The Royal Arch in the United States, is more dramatic in its form than that of England or Canada, yet in essentials it is the same.

The Order of the Temple in the English Ritual is brief; in the Canadian Ritual it is more elaborate and has its military features; in the United States it is more wordy, possibly more ornate and dramatic, yet it is essentially the same in all these countries.

The Rituals of the Order of Malta in these countries are so near alike that a person that is conversant with one can readily use the other; even a casual observer can readily see that this so-called "York Rite" in essentials is the same everywhere where the English language is spoken. The Concordat adopted in 1910 by the Temple Powers of the World, emphasizes this great fact.

The name "York Rite" is an inexcusable blunder; at least an unfortunate mistake. There never was a York Rite. It is unnecessary to enter upon any discussion as to the claims of the York Grand Lodge or a York system of Freemasonry as the question has been settled beyond controversy. The name "York Rite" is an inheritance from the forefathers of Freemasonry in the United States, who were more skilled in ritual tinkering than in the history of Freemasonry. This becomes especially apparent, when one remembers that the ephemeral Grand Lodge of York never chartered a single Lodge in America. The Freemasonry of the United States began under the Provincial Grand Lodge of Massachusetts, then under the Grand Lodge of England (*the Moderns*) with Price as Grand Master. The Grand Lodge of England (*the Ancients*) and the Grand Lodge of Scotland chartered Lodges in America, and it is reasonably possible, that before the union of the two Grand Lodges of England, the Royal Arch and the Masonic Orders of Christian Knighthood were conferred in this Country by the Military Lodges connected with the Irish Regiments stationed in the Colonies. To sum it all up, our so-called York Rite is the English Rite dressed in more fantastic clothing.

The name "York Rite" should be eliminated and the name English Rite substituted. In view of the foregoing facts as to what constitute a Rite, we in the United States are practicing or have formulated an American system of the English Rite; not an American Rite as it is frequently erroneously called, but a system of Degrees of the English Rite; it should be known as the English Rite, or Anglo-Saxon Rite.

Masonic Tradition and the Royal Arch

By Arthur Edward Waite

The old distinction between Blue and Red has almost fallen into disuse, so far as normal parlance is concerned, among members of the Craft in England; but we know that a memorial remains among us in the colour-symbolism found in the ROYAL ARCH. The Blue also connotes Symbolical Masonry, and this is a valid qualification, because the Third Degree opens a door into a great figurative Mystery as into the blue distance. It is not of our concern now or we might dwell for a moment on the significant fact that in Irish Craft workings the Candidate is told invariably that even the official and conventional penalties of the Three Degrees are to be regarded as a part integral of the symbolism which rules in all.

The ROYAL ARCH, or Red Masonry, has passed by its hypothesis out the symbolical domain: on the surface, at least, it is dealing no longer with allegory, but with an actual historical event. According to that version of the Holy Order which is at work in England and Wales, under the obedience of the Supreme Grand Chapter, it belongs - as we are all well aware - to the time of Zerubbabel and the building of the Second Temple. With certain variations, which are not essential in character, it is the same, I believe, in Scotland and the United States. In Ireland the historical time of the Grade is much later, being that of Josiah the King, but of this I am unable to speak except by report, as there are no Rituals available. There is a sense, however, in which all differences draw to the same end, for all are concerned with the central fact of a Secret Tradition, perpetuated by its hypothesis from an immemorial past, derived originally from sources behind Masonry and carried from Degrees leading up to the ROYAL ARCH, through the Holy Order itself and thence into Christian and some other High Grades. It is a remarkable fact that on the surface of the Craft Degrees there is practically no intimation of this traditional inheritance. The presumable explanation is that those who constructed the Legend of the Third Degree, following any vestiges which may have come into hands of the 18th Century from the part of York or Scotland, had a mind to follow - a little roughly and crudely the lines of the Ancient Mysteries concerning figurative death and resurrection. A signal confusion followed, for they slew the prototypical Master, whereas they raised the Candidate, creating a complete fissure in the logic of symbolism. So it has remained among us, but something like sixty years after the approximate date of construction, the Loge de la Bienfaisance at Lyons, which transmuted the RITE OF THE STRICT OBSERVANCE, intervened to save the situation, so far as French Masonry was concerned, and in the Grade of PERFECT MASTER of St. Andrew they raised Hiram as Christ. If we pursue the subject of confusion from another point of departure, we know that - by the hypothesis of the Third Degree - the Temple of Solomon was left unfinished, like the legend itself, from which consideration of simple fact it follows that any completion of the Third Degree should take up the Hiramic myth at the point where its story broke off, and lead it to an end in symbolism. Now we are familiar, and more than familiar, with the affirmation concerning the ROYAL ARCH, which is (1) that it is not to be regarded as in any sense a further Degree superposed upon the Craft, but (2) rather as a completion of the whole. So far, however, from concluding the Hiramic myth it leaves unabridged in Ritual a gap of several centuries, understood as historical time, and jumps to an examination of certain legendary events connected with preliminaries to the building of the Second Temple in the days of Zerubbabel. It follows that the Third Degree - historically speaking - is a story without an end, like Canova's German romance, while the ROYAL ARCH is a prolegomenon to another story, which story is not to be found in Masonry.

The sense in which the one is supplementary to the other is a matter of the Secret Tradition, a formula of loss and recovery, according to which the Holy Order seeks to elevate the Craft out of a region of untinctured symbolism to the threshold of Divine Science. It could have been done in a logical manner, preserving all the unities, and it so happens that the necessary elements were ready to the hands of the symbolists, if we can suppose as I think, is possible - that certain so-called side grades, or steps, were already existing in some primitive form. In this case the ROYAL ARCH has been lifted out of a sequence to which it belongs essentially, and apart from which its real message is divided and confused, if it must not be called lost. My purpose is to collect the links of the broken chain and then join them up. If the question be why does the Craft Candidate pass through a figurative experience which connotes the idea of death, and then through a shadow of resurrection, the answer is that the god died and rose in the

Ancient Mysteries, as in the great proto typical example which is that of Osiris. He was of the Divine Pantheon, and he returned thereto, as to former companions at once of toil and attainment. So also Iacchos was torn to pieces, but again he was restored to life; Tammuz died and rose; the dead Adonis was given back to the arms of Venus, even as Persephone to Demeter. If it be asked, on the other hand, why in the ROYAL ARCH there is a quest followed ad interiora terra and a discovery consequent thereon, the answer is that this is precisely the thesis concerning the preservation of a Secret Tradition, which descended from Adam, of which Enoch was a notable custodian, which came down to the time of Solomon and is carried thereafter through several eloquent memorials of Masonic Rite. It was not invented by Masonry, and if I speak here only of the mythos in Israel it is not peculiar thereto, though it appears under other aspects in other regions of traditional lore. Before linking up briefly the chain of Ritual, it is necessary to make a proviso with respect to the sources.

They are texts of what I am accustomed to call the Greater Exile of Israel, being that of the Christian centuries, and they are three in number: (1) The TALMUD BABLI; (2) The TALMUD HIEROSOLYMAE, and (3) The SEPHER HAZOHAR. The last is the latest of all in respect of time, its final reduction being referred by scholarship to the 13th Century, though it contains old elements. It is the great text of the Secret Tradition in Israel, and this - according to the ZOHAR - began with Adam, for Latin theology and that which is termed Kabalism meet unawares, and seem to clasp hands over things appertaining to the hypothetical state of unfallen man in Paradise. It was in a state of supernal know ledge, of the science which - by the theosophical hypothesis - has its root in the Tree of Life, in the unity of Divine things, not in the duality and sophistication which is referable to the Tree of Knowledge. It is said that when the Holy One, blessed be He, created Adam, He exhorted him to advance in the path of goodness and revealed to him the Mystery of Wisdom. Adam contemplated, indeed, all wisdom and all highest mysteries. He was "encompassed by the glory from on high," and was intended in the scheme of divine things to be united for ever with God, in Whose Image he had been made. But from the path of the Good and the One - all this notwithstanding - Adam fell into ways of separation and abandoned the Tree of Life, meaning the supreme theosophy of the inward Secret Doctrine. The penalty of this separation is described under the term death in the text of Genesis.   By the hypothesis of the ZOHAR, the Secret Doctrine, the Supreme Wisdom, in a word, that Hidden Treasure which was transmitted in perpetuity thereafter as a tradition through the ages, was communicated to the First Man by means of a book, which came down from heaven in the hands of the angel Raziel, and was delivered to Adam, the messenger in question being denominated Chief of Supreme Mysteries. It remained in the possession of Adam till he was driven out of the Garden, when it was ravished out of his hands. But as it is obvious that there could have been no Secret Tradition - such as was conceived by the mind of Israel - unless its depository were restored, so we hear in due course that in answer to his tears and entreaties it was given back in the end to our progenitor by the angel Raphael. Adam transmitted it to Seth, from whom it passed to Enoch, who, after he was taken by God became the great angel Metatron, the Angel of the Presence and Chief of the Celestial School. It is said that the School of Metatron is the School of the Holy One, and that in his hands are the Keys of Heaven. It came about for these reasons that the Secret Book is called the BOOK OF ENOCH, though it passed down ultimately to Abraham. Thereafter the ZOHAR is silent regarding its travels and whereabouts, but the Secret Tradition of which it is the source was communicated to the elders by Moses and thence, in the myth concerning it, through succeeding generations to the doctors of the Zoharic school, the chief repository at the time of the fall of Jerusalem being Rabbi Simeon ben Yochai. From Zoharic Kabalism the tradition descended to the follies and iniquities of Jewish Ceremonial Magic, and so it comes about that in these dregs and lees there is a BOOK OF RAZIEL, which is a book of Divine Names and Conjurations based thereon. It is a favourable specimen of its class, in comparison with Keys of Solomon, texts of Goetia, Sworn Books of Honorius and things under the generic title of Grimoires; but it presents a corrupted form of the tradition concerning Enoch. Antecedent to the ZOHAR, as I have intimated, are certain Talmudic fables, which exceed the scope of this notice. Antecedent to both are Josephus and a comparatively ancient apocrypha of the apocalyptic class under the name of the BOOK OF ENOCH. To Josephus we owe the well-known myth concerning the Pillars of Stone and Brick, on which Enoch inscribed the Mysteries of Knowledge belonging to the age before the Flood: there are many variations of the legend, which concerns broadly the perpetuation of the Secret Tradition. It is not otherwise to our purpose. But the BOOK

OF ENOCH, which is a series of visions beheld by the prophet when he was in the spirit, like the seer of Patmos, is a prototype of Masonic tradition and that especially which is reflected into the ROYAL ARCH. It is said that GOD shewed Enoch nine vaults in a vision, and that with the assistance of Methuselah his son, he proceeded to erect in the bosom of the mountain of Canaan a secret sanctuary, on the plan of what he had beheld, being vaults beneath one another. In the ninth, or under-most vault, Enoch placed a triangle of purest gold, on which he had inscribed that which was presumably the heart, essence and centre of the Secret Tradition, the True Name of God, comprehending all grace, all power and the providence of Divine Mercy. It is the development of this legend which can be followed through several Grades and various Rites of Masonry, the root of all therein being referable to the Traditional History in the Third Craft Degree. We know that which it was attempted to wrest by violence from the keeping of the Master Builder: we know what he died to preserve inviolable, and though in reality it did not perish with him - because there were other Keepers - we know that Masonry suffered a loss through the centuries, and is represented as in the quest of its discovery in the Opening and Closing of the Lodge in the Master Grade. We know in fine what substitutes were accepted as distinctive tests, to prevail everywhere, until in some manner as yet unknown the term of quest should be reached and the pearl of great price restored. When Moses, Aholiab and Bezaleel sat in the Holy Lodge, at the foot of Mount Horeb, during the long wanderings of Israel in the desert of Sinai, by the great hypothesis of the tradition, they were in plenary possession of all the Masonic treasures. When

Solomon and others of the triad, who ruled the Sacred Lodge, sat on Mount Moriah, it was still as if the sun were at its meridian, a noon-tide glory of Masonry. But a change came over, by which the triad was broken and the light of the Art was obscured. It seems to me that in the deeper understanding our Craft Lodges are a memorial of this original loss: it is a logical inference from all that we are told in the story and from that which we claim to seek; for it is with us as it was with those Brethren of old, who, after the passing of the Master-Builder, agreed - till they could do better - to be content with things casual, though they desired things essential, and with accidents in place of the nominal. It is as if, having heard and followed a great call, and been long on the quest of God, it came about that - for want of a term - we had to rest satisfied with His image, or with unconsecrated Bread and Wine in place of the Higher Eucharist and the Holy Grail.

Freemasonry is founded on the immutable laws of Truth and Justice and its grand object is to promote the happiness of the human race.
   --WASHINGTON

But after nearly five hundred years - I am speaking still within the hypothesis of the symbolism - there rose up the Grand or Royal Lodge, which was in the day of restoration and the day when things are reborn, or made anew, when Zerubbabel, the prince of the people, with their prophet and priest, led back Israel out of exile. It came about that, having made a great discovery within the precincts of the First Temple, they held their Lodge at Jerusalem, and proclaimed the glad tidings, which are called the climax of

Freemasonry - at least within the measures and under the obedience of the Old Law. And the original of that which we term the ROYAL ARCH is the Grand or Royal Lodge. In the sense of this symbolism, notwithstanding all disparities occasioned by things that are left at a loose end and all temporal lacunae, it may be said that the Holy Order does, within its own degree, complete the Masonic circle - though only within measures of the Craft - in virtue of that mystical recovery which made the glory of the Third Grand Lodge even as the glory of the first, and Jerusalem in the days of Zerubbabel as Horeb in those of Moses, who first promulgated the beneficent Law of Masonry. The ROYAL ARCH may be defined briefly as the Grade of the Word attained; but while a certain expectation is intimated on the part of those who ruled, there is nothing to show that the Brethren who made the discovery were qualified by antecedent knowledge or were themselves dedicated to the work of quest. It was the providence of an accidental happening which brought about the event, and as such - on the surface - it does little honour to the important subject in hand.

The discovery itself is unintelligible, as the story stands, since there is nothing leading up thereto - either in the Craft or Arch. But in Masonic Grades external to both the preliminary steps are found and the motive at work throughout. In view of this fact, as explained already, it would look as though the ROYAL ARCH had been lifted out of some Ritual series and utilized as an epilogue to the Craft, not a little to its own detriment, because it was never intended originally to stand alone. In Masonic history we hear of the bare title and of some un-described symbol belonging thereto being carried in a Masonic procession, tempus 1743, while a year later there is an allusion to the Grade itself, but under circumstances which suggest that more than one version was about. The preliminary sidesteps or intermediates to which I have alluded and which throw light on the subject are not in distinct evidence till a later period.   If I may put forward a personal opinion, purely at its hypothetical value, it seems to me that as the ROYAL ARCH originated in these islands, certainly and beyond question, so also there were other Grades, side-steps or preliminaries connected therewith and essential thereto. It is impossible to speculate about their original form, in the absence of all evidence, or on how far they have departed from it in the Degrees now extant: if we may judge by the vicious editing of the Arch Degree itself, they have suffered drastic change. The Grades in question are called respectively ROYAL and SELECT MASTER. But before offering a brief description of their scope and motive I must refer to the year 1754, when several important items were grouped together under the auspices of a French Rite, as if they had been manufactured suddenly or suddenly collected together.   I refer to the COUNCIL OF EMPERORS OF THE EAST AND WEST, otherwise the RITE OF HEREDOM or RITE OF PERFECTION, working twenty-two Grades superposed on those of the Craft. In virtue of certain sub-titles attached to some of them on the authority of rare MSS. now in my hands, it would appear that not all of them were of French Origin, though it is impossible to have any assurance on such a debatable point. The examples include ENGLISH MASTER, as alter native to INTIMATE SECRETARY, and ILLUSTRIOUS IRISH MASTER, as substitute for PROVOST AND JUDGE. However this may be, we are concerned more especially with the thirteenth Grade of the Rite, called ROYAL ARCH OF ENOCH, or - in early examples - Knight of the ROYAL ARCH. As there are two titles, so also there are two forms and that which is the more important is, I think, perhaps the later: it is incorporated at the present day into the long series of the SCOTTISH RITE. It goes very near to the root-hypothesis of the Secret Tradition and delineates the circumstances under which the Sacred Word was placed in the hiddenness, long prior to the Three Prototypical Grand Lodges. In this form, I believe, it to be of foreign invention as well as redaction: its importance for our purpose is that it places a Masonic complexion on an early epoch of the Tradition. In the alternative and possibly earlier form there is no question that it is of English origin as to its root-matter or that it derives from the ROYAL and SELECT MASTER GRADES, but from the former more especially, and at a time when both were in a state corresponding more nearly to the mode in which they were communicated, not so many years ago, under the auspices of the EARLY GRAND Scottish Rite, rather than that of the CRYPTIC. The latter bears marks of editing by persons who had no acquaintance with the Secret Tradition. As regards all recessions, the time is that of Solomon, the Temple is still uncompleted, but the mythical history in each case is subsequent to the Hiramic myth, which is still left at its original loose end. The Grades in their several forms throw light on the central point of the Royal Arch, because they shew how a place of concealment was planned for the Secret Mysteries and how these were hidden therein until time or circumstances should render their restoration essential. The implicit throughout is that in such case the providence protecting what is understood as Masonry would intervene in favour of the Art, as it did ex hypothesi at the epoch of the Second Temple. We may follow the Secret Tradition into strange places of Masonry, and if the intimations are often at variance they are in agreement on at least two points. The Tradition is always concerned with the power and grace of a Word, usually a Divine Name, and there is always an intention to show that a hidden Knowledge concerning it goes on from age to age. There is the Grade of KNIGHT OF THE EAST, which in one of its versions belongs to the Maccabean period, and the Candidate is in search of the Sacred Treasure after the profanations of Andochus Epiphanus. There is the Grade of TRUE SCOTTISH MASTER, which belongs to Adonhiramite Masonry. It affirms that the Word of God was never lost in reality, and that after the sacking of Herod's Temple, at the destruction of Jerusalem by Titus, a mysterious inscribed plate was found beneath one of the Pillars. This fable is recited in a kind of historical discourse, and although on the surface we are still in the days of Solomon, we are already on the threshold of Christian Masonry, for the Lodge of the Grade is said to have been instituted by St. John the Evangelist in succession to one which was held on the banks of the Jordan by St. John the Baptist. When we pass definitely into Christian Masonry the Tradition is still with us, although under several mutations. It owes something to Philostorgus and his ECCLESIASTICAL HISTORY, written at the beginning of the 5th Century. In connection with the baffled attempts to rebuild the Temple at Jerusalem he tells us of certain workmen let down by means of ropes into a deep well, at the bottom of which - emerging above the water - there was found a small column, and on the column, a book wrapped in a linen cloth. When examined, it proved to be a copy of St. John's Gospel. For the rest, according to Christian Masonry, the Keepers of the Secret Tradition are represented as Knights of the Morning, Knights of Palestine, Sons of the Valley, Thebaid Brethren, a secret Brotherhood perpetuated from generation to generation in the heart of Jewry, but unknown to Jewry at large. They looked for a Master who was to come, the Deliverer and Messiah. In the fullness of time they found the Word in Christ, which is the message of the Christian Grades.   I have been dealing with questions of fact in Ritual and with the tradition out of which they arise. I do not intend on the present occasion to dwell on the inferences to be drawn, however legitimate. I have followed the Secret Tradition in its development through several paths, within and outside of Masonry. That there is a meaning behind the Tradition I am entirely certain, for it is of symbolism or allegory after its own manner and within its own measures, even as Masonry is..   The great BOOK OF THE ZOHAR contains the whole doctrine of the Lost Word and of the circumstances under which it shall be restored on the coming of Israel out of exile, in the day of Messiah. But the ZOHAR is the book of the Secret Tradition in Jewry under the Christian aegis. As regards the Lost Word, it depends from a question of fact, which of itself is of minor consequence, being the loss of the mode in which the High Priest pronounced the Divine Name when he entered the Holy of Holies once a year to make atonement for the sins of the people. Over this the ZOHAR allegorizes and in their fervid hearts the doctors of the Greater Exile looked for magnalia Dei when it should be put again into their mouths. But that which it meant in their symbolism was the coming of the Kingdom of God on earth - to the chosen people above all, but apparently by derivation from these to all tongues and tribes and peoples and nations. The Secret Tradition was taken over by zealous scholars of Christendom during the 16th and 17th Centuries, and they sought to convince Jewry that all which was expected had come in Christ, that it was possessed by the Gentiles and might be enjoyed by them if they would turn their hearts to Him. This is the philosophy of the Tradition in brief and crude summary. But in another form and aspect, it is the philosophy of the Tradition in Masonry, which is another story of a Word in loss or hiddenness, and this fact, which might be one of coincidence, is linked up with the Secret Tradition because it is represented - in variably and only - by a Sacred Name, an omnific and ineffable message, and the plenary grace of a mystery abiding in a Name of God. Now the Tradition of the Name in Masonry was taken over by other Zelatores, who, after all intimations of the ROYAL ARCH OF ENOCH, Arch of Zerubbabel and Arch of Josiah the King, after all that was said to be inscribed on sacred plates of gold, came forward in their later day and founded the Christian Grades - the ORDER OF THE TEMPLE, the ROSE CROIX, the RED CROSS OF CONSTANTINE and KNIGHT OF THE HOLY SEPULCHRE. Like other makers of legend, they testified that the Word is Christ. It follows that those rumours of a Secret Tradition which are conveyed in the Royal Arch are not confined thereto. In one or other form, they are in the body-general of Masonry. What does this fact signify, and where may it lead the Mason who is willing to dwell on such things and, perhaps, pursue them further? The answer to this question is my last word and a kind of obiter dictum. It signifies that the Secret of Masonry, that Word too often lost, is the Secret of Christ realized in the heart of a Mason, and that from beginning to end our "peculiar system of morality, veiled in allegory and illustrated by symbols " has never had another object than to direct us with eyes uplifted to the bright Morning Star, whose rising brings peace and salvation to those who sit in tribulation and in the shadow of death.

High Purpose and Genius of Royal Arch Masonry

By William F. Kuhn

AS General Grand High Priest, I am endeavoring to visit as many Grand Chapters as possible during my term of office, and I have but one theme: more dignified and impressive ritualism and a moral and educational value of the Capitular degrees. It is a lamentable fact that Royal Arch Masonry has not come into its own. Many Freemasons are proud of the fact that they are Master Masons, or Knights Templar, or Scottish Rite Masons, but seldom do they boast of being Royal Arch Masons. There must be a reason for this, and it lies in the fact that Capitular degrees have been conferred in an undignified manner, and the moral, historical and educational value have been entirely neglected. But a change is coming, and these degrees are receiving more attention and a more dignified rendition than ever before. It has been established beyond a doubt that even the most light-headed of men prefer dignified work and an occasional glimpse of the moral and intellectual values contained therein.

Royal Arch Masonry will come into its own as soon as these facts are recognized. Freemasonry is a beautiful allegory, which unfolds to the thinking Freemason, the interesting story of the Loss, the Recovery and the practical application of that which we call the Word. This is all that the great textbook, Freemasonry, contains. The Loss is symbolized in the lodge, and the Recovery, with its practical application to life, is symbolized in Royal Arch Masonry. Freemasonry has a golden thread, a central idea running through all of the degrees and around which all the symbolism of Freemasonry revolves. This central idea, or the goal of Freemasonry, upholds the entire fabric, and unless this is kept in mind, the whole structure falls to the ground. This center is the Master's Word.

Freemasonry is not a lot of degrees piled one upon another without any connecting link, or a heterogeneous mass gathered together with the mere idea of fooling the candidate into taking many degrees. But there is this goal running through Ancient Craft Masonry of which the Capitular degrees are an important part thereof. The non-recognition of this fact has prevented Royal Arch Masonry from coming into its own. It has been misunderstood, misinterpreted and made a jest, instead of recognizing the greatest field for intellectual and moral development of anything in Freemasonry. This co-relation of the degrees of Ancient Craft Masonry was recognized by the United Grand Lodge of England when it stated that "*Ancient Craft Masonry consists of the degrees of Entered Apprentice Fellow Craft, Master Mason, together with the Holy Royal Arch*," and in the second section, it declared "*that the lodges may confer the Orders of Chivalry under their several constitutions.*"

IT IS A PART OF ANCIENT CRAFT MASONRY

This means that the Royal Arch Degree is a part of Ancient Craft Masonry, and the Orders of Chivalry were recognized as Masonic. This constitutes York Rite Freemasonry. It naturally follows that one degree is not higher than another, but is a part of the unfolding of an interesting story, and the Royal Arch is as much a part of Ancient Craft Masonry as the Master's Degree, and it may be truthfully stated that no one is in possession of all of Ancient Craft Masonry without the Royal Arch. In this interesting relation and co-relation we have the beautiful symbolism of the Loss, the Recovery and the interpretation of the Master's Word. If there is a Loss there must be a Recovery, and the Recovery is of little value unless you interpret the Recovery. It would be merely theoretical, philosophical nonsense to discover the Master's Word, and fail to interpret it in a practical application to our duties as Freemasons.

The Royal Arch portrays this Recovery. That is, you receive the degree in a manner that will enable you to recognize that you have made the Discovery. Unfortunately, many who have received the Royal Arch Degree did not receive anything and the whole thing was merely a joke. Many newly-made Master Masons have been disappointed in not receiving that which was promised them, and in the fact that they were put off with a substitute, although they received the promise that at the proper time the true Word should be discovered.

Originally, the Word may have been given in the Master's Degree, but the introduction of the legend of Hiram Abiff necessarily made a fourth degree possible. Not only made it possible but absolutely necessary to symbolize the Recovery. This is the story of Freemasonry. The candidate feels a disappointment in not receiving the Master's Word as had been promised him, but he fails to grasp the truth behind this denial, this disappointment, but when he analyzes the question from every angle and side he will invariably come to the conclusion that he was unprepared and unqualified to receive it. Men are not qualified to receive great truths instantly. It has been stated that a great truth requires three hundred years before it is accepted. The philosophy and history of religion bear out this idea. It is a lamentable fact that great truths, throughout the ages, have found unqualified ears. This is true of ancient Babylon, of Persia and Egypt. It is true of the Hebrew nation. All have been searching for truth. They have been reaching out. They have been grasping for it. All the prophets of the Hebrew people, from Moses to Malachi, and even including many great men of modern times, have spoken words and taught truths that fell upon unqualified listeners and deaf ears. It is the old, old history, of rejection, because not understood. It requires years of discipline, research and intellectual toil before arriving at the stage of being qualified to comprehend great truths in their completeness. The Master Mason did not receive that which was promised him, because he was not qualified in those things that "*Mark the perfect man.*"

We are searching for the truth, the Master's Word, and this search is evolutionary, constantly rising to a higher and better conception. This is well illustrated in the conception of Jehovah from that of Abraham down to the time of Christ. Every prophet took an advanced step in his conception of Deity and the Tribal God of Moses became the Father Omnipotent and loving to all who worshipped Him.

FREEMASONRY IS A GREAT SCHOOL

Freemasonry is a great school in which every Freemason, if he desires, may educate himself. He will not only be a historian, but a Bible student. If he is a reader he will find the footprints of Freemasonry in all history, in the arts and sciences.

The chapter degrees illustrate symbolically and teach four important and necessary lessons, which he who seeks that which was lost who would make the recovery, must have in his heart and soul. Without the possession of these attributes no recovery will ever be made and that which was lost will forever remain in darkness.

Every Freemason is symbolically a workman, whether his place is in the quarries or shop. Every day finds him standing before the Overseers to test the work wrought by him, according to the design laid down in the "Great Trestle Board." These designs require good work, and square work, because only good work and square work can be used in the building of the temple. A square man, and a square man only; a man who stands foursquare to the world, not a trickster, a politician, a doughface, or a weathervane, is demanded. A man who can face the world unshaken, unashamed, a bold uncompromising man for all things right, is needed everywhere. In the great search for that which was lost, such a man has taken a long step on his journey.

One of the great essentials today is to have an open mind. You and I are too bigoted in many things. We have our set ways, our set way of thinking. You remember that when a beautiful stone was presented, it was rejected because it did not fit the square of the Overseer, and they heaved it over among the rubbish. The trouble has been in the past, and is today, a great hindrance to progression, that we are all carrying about little dinky squares and every time anything new comes up we put our squares to it, our notion of the thing, not our reason, but chiefly a notion and conception, and if it does not fit the little squares of ours, we heave it among the rubbish. We do not stop to analyze the question. We have a preconceived notion, not an idea, hence we throw the new thing overboard. This is true in politics; it is true in religion, it is true in science. In fact it is true in everything that is new. This is the story of the Master's Word. Everything new that comes we meet it in a defensive manner. We do not canvass it and examine it, but without thinking about it, reject it. We are not open- minded.

I do not believe that any man can discover the Master's Word who is a bigot, who is not willing to weigh things. We know what bigotry has done in this world; that it has kept churches apart and has made partisan politics. A Freemason ought to be a man with an open mind, willing to analyze anything that comes along, from the humblest to the most scientific. We have heard a great deal about the fundamentalists and the liberals in religion. The fundamentalist backs up and says, "No, that is not according to my notion; I will reject it." The liberalist takes everything that comes along, fails to analyze it well enough to see whether it fits or not. You have heard of a distinguished citizen who was scared to death for fear that somebody would find that his grandfather was a monkey. It is being said that on account of science men are doubting the

Bible and rejecting it. This is a purely unthinking, superficial view. My advice is, read all the scientists and all the higher criticism, then analyze them and think it over. I know where you will land. There is no danger to the thinking man of becoming an atheist. All the criticism and all the scientific books, all the theories of creation, when we apply them intelligently and correctly, make the Bible stronger than ever. That which was mere faith before now is substantiated by reason. Do not be afraid of higher criticism. Do not be afraid of the so-called sciences. If the religion you have cannot stand the test of true and proven science, it is not worth very much. Religion will meet all scientific truth and meet it in the proper spirit and in the proper way. It may change some of our preconceived notions, but laying aside these notions, your religion will come out stronger and better than ever. I am not afraid about evolution. I believe in evolution. I cannot see the flowers in the front yard without making me believe in the principles of evolution. These beautiful flowers were once weeds. The process of evolution has made them what they are now. So with everything. But evolution does not necessarily mean monkeyism at all. Even if it did, behind it all stands the fiat, created. We cannot get away from that. I do not care whether this world was made in seven days or whether it took billions of years. Back of it all stands the world, created. So far as the monkey is concerned, if we are evolved from the monkey then it is a fine type of evolution and we must congratulate the monkey. Of course, a great many people are afraid of having their ancestry exposed, and I do not blame them, but the world does not care a fig as to who your grandfather was, but it is asking, "*Who are you, what are you going to do?*" Even the monkey evolution is not nauseating, as I would rather have a good clean monkey for my great, great, great grandfather than some people I know.

A Freemason ought to look things squarely in the face, lay aside his prejudice, and study the question carefully. There is nothing to be afraid of. Let us lay aside our dinky squares and recognize the beautiful and not heave it over among the rubbish because we do not understand it. There are many things that have been thrown in the rubbish heap that in after years were discovered as the most beautiful and important things. Men have lived, wrought hard, and died rejected. It took years before their work was recognized, and they stand today as remarkable men in the history of nations of the world. An open- minded man is never a partisan. It is all right to belong to a party; but it is all wrong to have a party own him, and he fail to exercise horse sense in analyzing questions. A Freemason ought to be an independent man, with no yoke about his neck. When Freemasons can analyze questions, consider them deliberately, come to a rational conclusion, they are coming closer to receiving the Master's Word.

THE SECOND LESSON IS SELF-CONTROL

The second lesson is that of self-control, obedience to constituted authority. This is taught in the Past Master's Degree. Of course, very few of you have seen this lesson in the degree. This degree is used chiefly in some Grand Jurisdictions as a means of making a fool of a man and, as conferred, is a disgrace to Freemasonry; yet it contains one of the fundamental principles of Freemasonry; that before a man will rule, he must first learn to obey; that before he would teach, he must first be a student; a Craftsman before he will be a Master of the Craft; a subject before he would be a king; and before he would enlighten others, he must become enlightened himself. These principles are fundamental, but the tendency of our present day is, that a man wants to be the boss before he is an Entered Apprentice; be Master of his lodge before he has been an obedient Craftsman. The world is suffering from unprepared men; unprepared for existing conditions; for an honest day's work; for adverse conditions that may arise, possessed of a mere smattering of everything, but little of anything; an expert in all things but an expert in nothing. Undisciplined men, men who lack self-control, are a curse of the age. A disregard of law, and incompetency to perform, is as prevalent among the better class as among the crooks. Bold defiance of law is everywhere present. Men wink at the violation of law, especially the eighteenth amendment. No Freemason will violate this law or wink at the violation thereof. If he does he will never find the Master's Word. A true Past Master has learned the lesson of obedience in the school of discipline, has become master of himself and is thoroughly prepared for the duties upon which he would enter.

There must have been supreme satisfaction to King Solomon to erect the magnificent and costly Temple of Jehovah. It represented all that the Oriental mind could conceive as an offering to God. The inspiring display that marked the preliminary step to, and the dedication of, the Temple is one of sublimity and glory. The inspired writer depicted it so graphically, describing this scene, touched the theme with more than mortal pen. Picture the Temple reflecting its golden splendor under the noon-day sun; imagine the great choir chanting antiphonally that wonderful psalm, "Lift up your heads, oh ye gates, and be ye lifted up, ye everlasting doors, and let the King of Glory come in." Listen to that inspiring prayer of the King, standing on the brazen scaffold in his rich and kingly robe, see the fire descend on the sacrificial altar, and the Temple illuminated by the Divine Presence, while the vast throng fall prostrate worshipping and praising. "For He is good, for His mercy endureth forever." Who would not like to have witnessed this wonderful scene?

But, has not the same scene been re-enacted in many a human heart? It may not have had the external splendor; it may not have been that of a King or Prince, but that of an humble man, who toiled daily, yet this individual, personally dedicated, partook of the same splendor, heard the same choir, uttered the same prayer, and beheld the fire descend on his meager sacrifice, and felt the glory of the Divine Presence. We are, indeed, Temple Builders. Some are building a magnificent temple. Some are building the best temple they can. Men differ in ability. Men differ in opportunities. But it does not matter whether you are building a little temple, building of bricks rather than granite, or bricks without straw, yet the temple is being built. You and I will have to complete our temple and the last stone must be put in position and may it receive the plaudits as of old, "Grace, grace be unto it."

Companions, do you not think that if a man is independent, does square work, and square work only, controls himself and is obedient to constituted authority, who is building a temple in this world, do you not think he is getting pretty close to the Master's Word?

THE PURPOSE OF THE WEARY SOJOURNERS

I have often thought of those three weary sojourners coming out of Babylonian captivity, making their long and toilsome journey from Babylon to Jerusalem with only one purpose in mind, and that was to rebuild the city and the House of the Lord. These three Jews were heroes but, while just released from captivity, it should be remembered that the great age of the Jewish nation was not in regal splendor in its solidarity as a nation, in its armies, in its wealth, or its expansive boundaries, but its golden age was the seventy years of captivity. It was the literary age of Jewry. Out of it came its sacred writings, the collation of its remarkable history of her people, her prophetic literature and her psalter. Had the captivity never occurred the world might have been denied its greatest heritage, the Old Testament. From the school of captivity emerged a people immortal, a people who were the creators of the sacred and undying literature of the world, and the steadfast adherence to Jehovah.

Note the purpose and aim of these three weary sojourners. A purpose that was never lost in their long and toilsome journey, on foot, over rough and ragged roads through desolation and amid ruins, but ever onward toward Jerusalem, the city of their fathers. The journey was not taken to secure ease, comfort, emolument or honor, but solely for the purpose of engaging in the noble and glorious work of rebuilding the city and House of the Lord. This truly was a noble purpose, but it did not embrace all, as they did not expect even "the hope of a fee or a reward." This was the climax of their noble purpose. It was unselfish. It was unstinted service, a service to their home, to their people and to their God. What greater encomium can be given to these faithful, devout, returning captives than to say they served? Any portion of the work, however humble, their willing hands were willing to perform. The keystone of the Royal Arch should bear upon it, "I Serve." Service, self-sacrifice, should be the battle cry of Freemasonry, and he who does not wish to serve or sacrifice, will never discover the Master's Word.

These three zealous Jews discovered it. They did not discover it in a palace but in a vault. They found it after digging away the rubbish, away from the sight of men, not for worldly applause or honor, but for pure service, and they found it.

This is the beautiful story of Freemasonry: The loss of the Master's Word and its recovery by men being fully prepared and qualified searching for it, and willing to make long and toilsome journey through life, with one end in view, to assist the noble and glorious work of building the House of the Lord, working for humanity without the hope of fee or reward. When Freemasonry grasps this idea, that it is a life service, a life of self-sacrifice, then will Royal Arch Masonry come into its own. When we grasp the idea of Royal Arch Masonry as I have tried to explain it, it will not any longer be a mere stepping stone from the lodge to the Commandery, but we shall consider it an honor to be Royal Arch Masons, and no higher honor can come to any man than to appreciate and understand Royal Arch Masonry.

Companions, many of you are High Priests of your Chapters, candidates are coming into your Chapters. Will you explain to them this story--that they are searching for eternal truth, or will you make these solemn ceremonies a scene of buffoonery? I sincerely hope not. These ceremonies are too sacred and it would be a sacrilege to introduce anything that is not in keeping with the dignity of Freemasonry. Shrine ceremonies have no place in Freemasonry and only the light-headed and the moron will indulge in it.

THERE HAS BEEN TOO MUCH RUSH

There was never a time in Freemasonry when this ought to be brought home with greater force. There has been a great rush into Freemasonry. There has been a hip and hoorah about it. Men have come having no conception of what Freemasonry is, but they are going to drop out. The tide is going out. Dimissions and suspensions for non-payment of dues will increase. What are you going to do with this vast amount of unthinking material? Among this material are many good men as well as a mass of driftwood. Many have come without qualifications.

Let me tell you a little story. During the Civil War, Senator Vance of North Carolina, one of the most brilliant men of the Southern States, being an active Confederate, was disfranchised by the government. After the war he was elected to the United States Senate. He went to Washington with his certificate of election and was informed that his election was all right, but having been disqualified, and this disability not yet removed, he therefore could not be seated. He was informed that if he would remain in Washington a short time, Congress would doubtless pass a bill removing his disability. But Senator Vance was determined to go home. In doing so he took an ordinary coach and a seat opposite two ministers, a Baptist and a Presbyterian. These two Dominies soon became engaged in a warm discussion on the question of foreordination and election. The war waged hotly between the Navy and Infantry of the Lord's Kingdom. After a while, the Presbyterian minister, noticing that Senator Vance was very much interested, said to him, "*Stranger, you seem to be interested in our discussion. What is your opinion of election?*" Senator Vance said, "*I have a very positive opinion. An election is not worth a damn until your disabilities are removed.*" This is a good Masonic as well as theological statement. Too many men have been and are still coming in whose disabilities have not been removed. They are here. What are you going to do about it? Are you going to educate them as Freemasonry ought to educate her young men, or are you going to let them drift and finally drop out by taking their dimits or by non-payment of dues? Every man is not fit to be made a Mason. There are some who naturally will drop out if Freemasonry is not congenial. We have moral morons as well as intellectual morons, and a moron is not fit to be made a Mason, whether he be one morally or intellectually. Will you help those that remain? Are you going to have a circus out of it, or are you going to be sincere and teach these men the great central thought of Freemasonry? Now, Companions, as Royal Arch Masons, will you please consider these things: that the Chapter means much. It is the great stepping-stone to the central idea, the Master's Word, the Recovery of it and its interpretation and application. It is not foolishness. It is sincere, dignified work, just as much as the church itself. I sometimes think that if we took Freemasonry sincerely, studied it, brought it out as I have tried to explain to you, it will lead every man to the door of the church.

The Fourth Degree

By William F. Kuhn

The Royal Arch stands as the rainbow of promise in the Ritual; it stands as the promise of the resurrection; of that which was lost and that it shall be recovered. The question arises as to whether the Master's Word was originally communicated in the Third Degree? On this point there is some diversity of opinion. In our present Ritual of the Third Degree the Master's Word is lost. Dr. Oliver, a noted Masonic historian, says: "The True Word was never lost but transferred to the Royal Arch," and in corroboration of this statement further says: "I have before me an old French engraving of the Ground Work of the Master's Lodge, dated in 1740, containing the usual emblems and on the coffin is the 'True Word' in Roman capitals." This would tend to prove that before the legend of Hiram Abiff was introduced into the Master's Degree, the True Word was communicated in the Master's Degree and not a Substitute Word. It necessarily followed that when the legend of Hiram became a part of the Ritual of this degree, the "loss" of the "Word" followed, as the "loss" is a part of the Hiramic legend. But the "loss" without a "recovery" would be an absurdity; to complete the symbolism of Freemasonry, the "Word" must be recovered, hence the necessity for a Fourth Degree, the Royal Arch.

In 1738, or earlier, the story of the loss of the Word and the new legend, the Royal Arch, were gradually introduced into the lodges, and when the division occurred, (1751) dividing the

Freemasonry of England into the "Moderns" and "Ancients," the latter organized a Grand Lodge and adopted a Ritual of Four Degrees, the fourth being the Royal Arch. The Grand Lodge of "Moderns" evidently continued to use the old Ritual, without the legend of Hiram Abiff, while the Grand Lodge of "Ancients" used the new Ritual containing the Hiramic legend and the Fourth Degree, until the year 1813, when the two Grand Lodges united and formed the present Grand Lodge of England, known as the United Grand Lodge of England. It is therefore to the Grand Lodge of Ancients that we owe the Master's degree as found in our Ritual and also the preservation of the Royal Arch Degree. One of the Articles of union of the two Grand Lodges of England in 1813 was the retention of the degrees as formulated by the Grand Lodge of "Ancients;" hence, among the articles of agreement of this union, we find the only declaration made anywhere or at any time as to what constitutes "Ancient Craft Masonry." This article declares that "*Ancient Craft Masonry shall consist of the degrees of Entered Apprentice, Fellowcraft and Master Mason, together with the Holy Royal Arch.*"

We see, therefore, that the Royal Arch is merely the evolution of a truth contained in the early Third Degree. It is not a "Higher Degree," but the last volume of the series in a sublime story revealed through symbolism. The Master's Degree without the Royal Arch is a story half told, a song unsung and a promise unfulfilled. The candidate is promised that he should receive, but is put off with a "Substitute." He is left in darkness, in doubt, and to the thoughtful one in a condition of disappointment. Yet, there is a purpose behind this seeming deception. Light and revealed Truth come only through toil and willing service. This lesson must be learned before any Mason is qualified to know and appreciate the Truth, The Master's Word. It is, possibly, unfortunate that the Royal Arch Degree was separated from the "*Blue Degrees*;" but whether fortunate or unfortunate, the Royal Arch stands as the last of the degrees in Ancient Craft Masonry. It is the summit and no Master Mason is in possession of all that Freemasonry teaches without the Royal Arch. The series of four degrees continued to be conferred under a lodge charter until about 1750, in America at least. The earliest history that we have of the Royal Arch in this country was in 1758, when it was conferred under a lodge charter in Philadelphia. It was introduced into New York about the same time by an English military lodge, in Massachusetts in 1869, where it was conferred by St. Andrew's Lodge.

Since that time the Royal Arch Degree has remained secure in its superior place. "*The term Royal Arch Lodge was succeeded by Chapter and Royal Arch Chapter. The word Chapter was used in Connecticut as early as Sept. 5, 1783; in Pennsylvania, Sept. 5, 1789, in New York, April 29, 1791; in Massachusetts, December 19, 1794. The word Chapter took the place of Lodge in England, for the first time, April 29, 1768. The word Companion, used in the Chapter in place of Brother, was first used in England in 1778. These terms, Chapter and Companion, were soon carried to America where they flourish as elements in the Capitular system of degrees.*"

Such, in brief, is the history of the Royal Arch Degree; its parentage is as legitimate as any of the degrees of Ancient Craft Masonry; it sprang from the introduction of Speculative

Freemasonry into Operative Masonry--the fruit of symbolism and allegory. To be a Master Mason is the highest and most honorable degree that any man can attain; it entitles him to all the rights and privileges of the Craft; all the accumulated so-called higher degrees do not add anything to his Masonic stature. The Royal Arch is a part of the Master's degree--the summit of its excellency. It is the privilege and should be the duty of Master Mason to complete the Masonic story, told in allegory and revealed in symbolism by receiving the Royal Arch.

Would you be enrolled as one living in that future generation that shall discover IT? Act now.

THE MARK MASTER DEGREE

The degrees of the Chapter are: Mark Master, Past Master, Most Excellent Master and Royal Arch. The origin of the Mark Degree is veiled in obscurity, like all Masonic degrees, but, like the others, it sprang into existence in the earlier period of Speculative Freemasonry.

It was customary for the operative Masons to select for themselves a Mark, to be placed upon every piece of work wrought by them. This was done in order to keep a check on each operative's work by the Overseers, and to facilitate the payment of wages. Each Mark was distinctive and the same Mark frequently descended from father to son through several generations.

These Marks may be seen today on the stones in the old cathedrals of Europe. Facsimile copies are reproduced in all Masonic histories. In Scotland, the operative Mason was required to register his Mark by the Shaw's Statutes issued in 1598. From this requirement of registration of the Mark, the Degree was evidently evolved.

The earliest record of the Mark Degree being conferred in Scotland bears the date of January 7, 1778. Yet this does not prove that the degree was not conferred at a much earlier date. These records also contain the information that the Mark Degree could not be conferred upon any one not having received the degree of Fellowcraft and Master. A report made to the Grand Lodge of Mark Master Masons of England states: *"There is probably no degree in Freemasonry that can lay claim to greater antiquity than those of Mark Man or Mark Mason and Mark Master Mason."*

The degree was conferred in Nova Scotia in 1784; in Connecticut in 1791; in New York in 1791 and in Boston in 1793. Like the Royal Arch, the Mark Degree was originally conferred in the Lodge. In the United States, the General Grand Chapter, R.A.M., issued Mark Lodge Charters up to 1853, when it was prohibited and the degree passed under Chapter control. In England the degree is under the control of the Grand Lodge of Mark Masons; in Canada and in Scotland the control is vested as in the United States.

The lessons of the degree are intensely practical, emphasizing the great requirement in life, viz.: Qualification and service.

THE DEGREE OF PAST MASTER

The general use of the term, Past Master, by the Craft, means one who has been elected, installed and served for twelve months over a regular Lodge. The general use of the term does not imply a separate degree, although in many lodges and formerly in Missouri, the honorary grade of Past Master is conferred upon Masters elect as a part of the ceremony of installation. This grade or degree was or is conferred only in the presence of Past Masters. The degree is the second in the series of the Chapter; hence arose the terms, Actual Past Master and Virtual Past Master, the latter meaning one who had received the degree in a Chapter but who had not been elected or served as Master over a Lodge. A Virtual Past Master is not entitled to recognition by the Grand Lodge as a Past Master.

The degree is an old one. We find the expression of Past Master used in 1771 and implied as one "*having passed the Chair through some ceremony.*" The Constitution of the Grand Lodge of England, 1723, speaks of the installed Master passing through certain "significant ceremonies." There can be no doubt as to the antiquity of the degree. It dates from the birth of speculative Freemasonry. The introduction of the degree into Capitular Masonry rests on the fact that, originally, the Royal Arch was conferred only on those who had been elected and presided over a Lodge as Master, but it was manifestly unjust to a large portion of the brethren to have such a restriction placed upon them and the Royal Arch; the following law of 1789 illustrates this fact: "*No brother can be exalted until he has been at least three years a Master Mason and has presided six months as Master of some regular warranted Lodge or has passed the Chair of Dispensation.*" This law shows the old restriction and the modification that was assuming shape, permitting others than actual Past Masters to receive the Royal Arch. An old law found in Harmony Lodge, No. 52, Philadelphia, 1799, states: "*That every brother who has not passed the Chair shall pay fourteen dollars, out of which the Dispensation shall be paid for; if he has passed the Chair for being exalted, eight dollars.*"

That is, an actual Past Master could receive the Royal Arch Degree for eight dollars, but one who has not received the Past Master's Degree must obtain a Dispensation from the Grand Master to receive it before he could be made a Royal Arch Mason and it cost fourteen dollars.

When the Royal Arch Degree passed from under the control of the Lodge and became a separate system, known as the Chapter, the prerequisite to the Royal Arch remained, viz.: The Past Master's Degree. The Virtual Past Master Degree became a part of the Chapter series. The reason for this prerequisite becomes apparent when the Lessons of this much abused, but beautiful, degree are studied and understood. The lesson of obedience to authority is proof against anarchy, and he who would teach must first learn to obey.

MOST EXCELLENT MASTER DEGREE

A lie well told and repeated constantly becomes a truth to credulous people. This applies to the oft repeated statement that Thomas Smith Webb fabricated the American system of Capitular Degrees and the Orders of the Commandery of Knights Templar. Any man having an ounce of brains, and would use that ounce, will find that the degrees of the Chapter and the orders of the Commandery were in existence and conferred nearly fifty years before Webb was born. The Most Excellent is frequently credited to his fertile brain, and so stated by some Masonic writers, but fortunately there is on record in Massachusetts and New York the date of Webb's birth and the dates on which he received all the Masonic Degrees. The dates go to show that the Most Excellent was known and conferred before Webb became a Royal Arch Mason.

The latter half of the eighteenth century was prolific in Masonic Degrees in France and England. The degrees of all Rites can date their birth from 1723 to 1760, and in the maze of names and titles of degrees we find a veritable jungle. In this period we find the Irish System embraced The Chair, The Excellent, The Super Excellent, The Royal Arch, The Knight Templar and the Prince Rose Croix. The Scottish System embraced: The Mark Master, The Past Master, The Excellent Master and the Royal Arch. St. Andrew's Chapter, Boston, worked the Irish System, except The Chair, from 1769 to 1797. After 1799 the Mark, Past, Most Excellent and Royal Arch were conferred. A prominent Masonic writer says of the change: *"This transition indicates and suggests that the Super Excellent Degree contained the marrow and something of the bone of the Most Excellent Degree."*

From 1791 the Most Excellent was a well-known degree and a part of the Capitular system. The Super Excellent of this period must not be taken for the Super Excellent appendant to the Council of Royal and Select Masters of today. The Most Excellent Degree is a fitting prelude to the Royal Arch, one of the most impressive degrees in its ceremonies and sublimely spiritual in its symbolism.

WHAT OF THE HOUR?

What of the hour in Freemasonry? Brighter, stronger, clearer. We often become discouraged and are inclined to be pessimistic; but amid all the errors and stumbling, a better day is dawning, when we shall see the beneficent labors of Freemasonry shinning in effulgent splendor. Freemasonry is growing in power and beneficence. As its immortal principles take root in the fallow soil of the human heart and mind, it buds and blossoms into the foliage of kindness and the Hesperidean fruit of charity toward all mankind. While the Masonic tramp may be seen on the beautiful highway of Freemasonry, there are many more today than ever, who are toiling in mind and heart in the treasure strewn mines of Freemasonry's realm.

Freemasonry today means more than negative plaudits and negative principles; but she stand preeminently as a living, growing, resistless power, whose end and aim is the exaltation of man and the glory of "*The I Am That I Am.*" Our ancient brethren journeyed from Babylon to Jerusalem--out of bondage into freedom--with one strong purpose in view. What was the desire so pre-eminent in their hearts? What was the foundation of the zeal that actuated them to undergo the trials and hardships of that weary journey? Let them speak: "*To aid in the noble and glorious work of rebuilding our City and Temple of the Lord.*" It was Work, Work, Work. Not idleness and ease.

Capitular Masonry

By William Potts George

Capitular Masonry is the second stage or section in Masonic progress. It suffers often, and is frequently too lightly esteemed as an intermediate series of degrees between Blue Lodge Masonry and Knight Templary. But it is full of meaning and contains within itself lessons fully as important as can anywhere be found.

Blue Lodge Masonry is confessedly imperfect. Its highest revelation is a substitute for that which is left for future generations to discover, and its highest utterance is a mournful plaint over that which is incomplete, and of one cut off before his life's great work was done.

The finishing of the first Temple is left for the Chapter to accomplish. In the earlier section there is a complaint of "no designs upon the trestle board." The workmen are at work on the rough ashlars. In the second section the work is brought up for inspection. Through ignorance it is at first rejected, but afterwards it is received and wages paid therefor.

Surely these lessons are those of the last great inspection of every man's work by the Almighty Grand Master—

"Who will try the blocks we offer With His own unerring square."

"He will reward every man according to his work." After work, wages. After labor, rest.

PAST MASTER'S DEGREE

In the Past Master's Degree we learn some lessons of how to preside over our companions with dignity and honor.

MOST EXCELLENT MASTER'S DEGREE

Then, in the Most Excellent Master's Degree, we are privileged to witness the completion of the first Temple, when the keystone fills the arch; when king and priests and subjects worship together around the sacred altar; when the sacred fire of the Shekinah descends and cloudy glory fills the place. This is certainly a "Most Excellent" degree, and one of whose execution my own Orient Chapter is justly proud and of which our Grand Chapter may be equally proud, because our present Grand High Priest was the one who enlarged the degree to a beautiful presentment more worthy of its great dignity and importance than that which had previously obtained.

In the Royal Arch Degree we learn still greater lessons; for there we recover that which was lost and there we build the second Temple. This degree takes us first among the ruins of the first Temple. There we learn the lesson that this human nature of ours is in ruins. Originally created upright, man fell from his first estate. He lost his primeval purity. His moral nature was stained by sin, and the harmonious relation between himself and his Maker was interrupted. This is a great truth of the individual as well as of the race. We lose our childish innocence. We all put forth our hand and pluck some kind of "forbidden fruit," and the penalty is to know good by evil. Personal contact with evil stains our moral nature. Our eyes are opened and we are conscious of sin in ourselves and others.

Like Adam and Eve, we strive to hide ourselves from God and good men among the trees of the garden. And from that garden of childish innocence we are expelled till the "seed of the woman shall bruise the serpent's head," and until:

"Some greater man restore us and regain That blissful seat."

Human nature, like that first Temple, is in ruins, and it is our duty to rebuild it. For this high duty we are taught, first, the great lesson of humility. That is the necessary condition of mind for the reception of any truth. We are to receive the doctrine as a "little child," and some times to "learn in silence and subjection."

In all the preceding degrees we have been received in an upright position, as man unfallen, but now, in order to contemplate the ruins, to rebuild the Temple, and to receive higher instructions, humility is a requisite condition. We are on our way to exaltation, and it is "whosoever humbleth himself shall be exalted."

In all our other Masonic experiences we have been alone. It is not good to be always alone, and as time rolls on, men are formed into companies. Now we find ourselves with other companions, who, though all in darkness, can help and cheer each other on the long and perilous journey. Before, we prayed alone, now we pray together, as we realize that divine guidance and help are necessary for every undertaking. Adam, unfallen, prayed. Angels and saints in heaven continually worship. So we now, as heretofore, pray to God at all the different stages of our journey.

The Holy Bible is still open on the altar, uttering its perpetual Masonic protest against the popery that would close it, and enforcing the first Masonic dictum, "Let there be light!"

Our next lesson is received before the Burning Bush in the desert, and we are reminded of the scene where the future leader of the Israelites received his great commission from God to deliver His chosen people from Egyptian bondage. By what name shall we know Him who thus reveals Himself to us, and interferes with our Egyptian relations and promises us an everlasting inheritance? We shall hear something about that name bye and bye. Now let us contemplate the scene where the great Lawgiver receives it first himself, and learn something of its meaning.

THE BURNING BUSH

The bush is burning, but is not consumed. What is the process that we call burning? It is not an annihilation of matter, but a change in that matter's relations and trans formation of its energies. If we study the geological his tory of this earth of ours, we find that its energy has been constantly transformed by this same process that we call burning. And, when we bury in the bosom of our mother earth "the temple of our body," that body is destroyed by the same process of spontaneous combustion, and heat is the active factor in the transformation of that body's energy.

From that Burning Bush, "the symbol of nature's flux and reflux, the death that bounds her life, the life she brings from death, always consuming yet never consumed," Moses heard the voice of God.

So we are taught that in the interminable transformations of energy; in the innumerable changes which this Universe has witnessed; in the immeasurable and, to many, the meaningless and; insoluble mutations of matter and of energy, there is the Divine Immanence, the Divine Superintendence, and the Divine Controlling. God in the Burning Bush and the sublime "I Am" that issued therefrom as expressive of His nature, told Moses, and through him all succeeding generations, that the many changes which they note are not the result of blind force, of unintelligent and undirected energy, but that amid all the powers of Nature there is a Supreme Intelligence, a directing Mind, and a controlling Will. There is an All-Wise Governor and Ruler superintending these giant forces and evolving there from His sublime and all-wise purposes. Man and nature are not alone, but God is everywhere and universally operating in and through what we call nature. And —

"Nature is but the name of an effect, Whose cause is God."

So the supreme lesson which Moses and his Hebrew successors, the poets, seers and psalmists of the elder time, the stern Elijah, the mild Elisha, the rapt Isaiah, the plaintive Jeremiah, the mystic Ezekiel, the captive Daniel, the royal singer of Israel and his wise son Solomon, with all the other prophets of the Captivity and the second Temple, strove to impress upon the Hebrew mind was the nearness of their God. It was the lesson that he is one whose domain is not confined to the far-off beginning or the dim and distant future. He is not the God who is merely over and above and beyond man. But he is the God who is every where present with man, the God whose universal energy is constantly executing His own laws; the God of the senate and the store, the forum and the factory, as well as the God of the Tabernacle, the Temple, and His own Most Holy Place. His is the sleepless eyes which beholds in every place the evil and the good. To this God of the Burning Bush, the bush which illuminates even where it destroys, but not consumes, all things are "naked and open." "God is, and God is the rewarder of them that diligently seek Him." In the clearer Christian Dispensation the same truth reappears. St. Paul declared on Mars' Hill to the Athenian philosophers that "in Him we live and move and have our being;" and the Great Teacher reveals to us the Divine Father who numbers the very hairs of our head, and without whom not even a sparrow shall fall to the ground, the Ever-Living God of an ever-living people.

    The first temple, with all its glory, splendor and magnificence, is destroyed. But the God of the Temple, the God who appeared in cloudy glory at its dedication, lives. The bush burns, but it is not consumed. The I Am abides through all generations, and a second Temple must be built for His worship. Who will go up to gaze upon the ruins of the dismantled city? Who will search among the ruins for that which may be left to remind us of the former glory, and to be a pledge of that which shall succeed? The seventy years of chastisement and captivity are over. The divine agent, the King whose "heart is in the hand of Jehovah," and whose name and mission were prophesied by Jehovah's servant years before his birth, Cyrus, the King of Persia, has issued the decree to rebuild the city and the Temple. Who will go up for this great mission?

Solomon and the two Hirams, who devised and constructed the first Sanctuary, are in their graves beneath the green acacia. But the God who was with Solomon and the two Hirams will be with Zerubbabel and his coadjutors. The workmen die, but the work must go on — "Instead of the fathers shall be the children;" instead of the first Temple the second Temple shall be built upon Mount Moriah.

Between Babylon, Persia and Jerusalem lies a rough and rugged road, encumbered by rolling rivers, broken bridges, and by the ruins of ancient cities. But the God who led Moses and the children of Israel through the other pathless desert, by the pillars of cloud and of fire, still lives, still controls opposing forces, and still leads His people on their way. Through much tribulation they shall enter the kingdom. Often shall they be footsore and weary, but he will renew their strength and guide them on their journey. They shall meet many obstacles, only to overcome them. They shall not be daunted by difficulties, but shall surmount them. Foes shall attack them as they proceed, but the King's permit is their password. By prayer and constant communication with Deity they shall renew their strength and regain their vigor. They gaze upon the ruins of Tadmor and Damascus, but these are not Jehovah's cities, and they pass them by. Presently, from an eminence, they gaze upon Jerusalem. It is Jerusalem, the royal city: Jerusalem with the surrounding hills; Jerusalem, the city of Melchisedec, of David, and of Solomon; Jerusalem, whither the tribes have aforetime gone up to worship; Jerusalem, whose name they have lisped at their mother's knee; Jerusalem, of whose magnificence their fathers oft have told them. "If I forget thee, Oh Jerusalem, may my right hand forget its cunning!"

But it is now Jerusalem dismantled; Jerusalem shorn of its glory; Jerusalem in ruins; Jerusalem, the abode of the wolf and the jackal. But it is also Jerusalem to be rebuilt; Jerusalem to be repopulated; Jerusalem to be re stored. It is that Jerusalem concerning which the decree of Cyrus, and the fiat of Jehovah, have both been uttered, it is the city of Jerusalem, to have once more a Temple, in which shall dwell the God of the Burning Bush. It is the Jerusalem for which in the "fullness of time" awaits a greater destiny and a nobler visitor in the person of Emmanuel, God with us. And the God who descended upon the altar of King Solomon; the God who was with Moses in the Burning Bush, that same God is with the pilgrims now.

Before we approach the seat of the Council let us learn a few lessons. And these are still lessons of the ever-living God.

Blue is an emblem of universal friendship and benevolence, and is indicative of the cerulean canopy of heaven, the overhanging arch of azure whose firmative spans all we know of the visible universe. We receive here another revelation of the name of the Self- Existent One, who continues immutable through all the aeons of eternity, and who, amidst all the becomings and changings of the universe, abides in His eternal now — "I Am That I Am." It is the name that Moses heard from the burning bush in the desert, and which will be with us through all the dispensations. "I Am." And all that you can see in the majestic blue firmative fretted with golden fire is but the manifestation of His glory, the living garment of Deity, the mirroring and crystalizing of the thoughts of the Infinite Supreme. "I Am That I Am," and "Certainly I will be with thee," are sufficient assurances to quell the heart of every opposing tyranny, and to give success to every laudable endeavor.

Pass on, ye working sojourners, and solve the mysteries of the future. Purple, made by a combination of blue and scarlet, indicates the harmony between these several degrees. And the names of Shem, Ham and Japhet are the names of the patriarchs who survived the flood. That deluge was the cataclysm, which destroyed and changed created nature; but amidst those mighty world convulsions, when the "fountains of the great deep were broken up," and every living thing apparently destroyed, the Eternal God abides. The bush is unconsumed, and Shem, Ham and Japhet, the divinely-protected survivors who had rid den over the raging waters in the ark of safety, realized in themselves the promises and contained in themselves the germs for repopulating the earth, and once more under the Eternal One's superintendence evolving from Chaos, Cosmos; from Confusion, Order, and from Discord, Peace.

Scarlet symbolizes fervency and zeal — fervency in the exercise of our devotions; zeal to help and benefit and bless mankind. And these two should always go together! This stage overleaps in its teachings some generations. But once more we meet with those who realize the divine presence. Of Moses, the emancipator, leader and lawgiver, we have already spoken. It was he who met his Master in the burning bush. It was he who held communion with the awful God alone upon the lightning-circled brow of frowning Sinai, when the people trembled and he could only draw near as "God spake" the great ten words to man.

We have met with Moses before.

Aholiab and Bezaleel are mentioned in Exodus xxxi: *"And the Lord spake unto Moses, saying: 2. See, I have called by name Bezaleel, the son of Uri, the son of Hur, of the tribe of Judah: 3. And I have filled him with the Spirit of God, in wisdom and in understanding, and in knowledge and in all manner of workmanship. 4. To devise cunning works, to work in gold and in silver and in brass. 5. And in cutting of stones, to set them, and in carving of timber, to work in all manner of workmanship. 6. And I, behold, I have given with him Aholiab, the son of Ahisamach, of the tribe of Dan, and in the hearts of all that are wise-hearted I have put wisdom, that they may make all that I have commanded thee."*

To Bezaleel and Aholiab then was given the divine inspiration to work and to become the God- directed artificers of the desert tabernacle, or the tent from behind whose curtains Jehovah manifested and declared his will and love to the chosen people. To all these three were given in their different capacities divine direction and divine assistance for the work they had to do. And our lesson is that, that same immutable, unchangeable Jehovah who was with them when they built the tabernacle or tent in the desert, will not forsake us as we go forward to build his own permanent Temple in the city of Jerusalem.

Let us go forward till we reach white, the symbol of purity and perfection. That pure color white is formed by a combination of all colors; and the lesson is that when every excellency is thus blended into one harmonious whole we have the emblem of completeness, and the completeness of human character is perfect purity. The names of Johnua, Zerubbabel and Haggai speak again to us in trumpet tones of the continuance of the divine presence and favor, and of divine help in the enterprise in which we are now engaged. Joshua is the High Priest of the Most High God. Zerub babel is the Prince of the royal house, to whom the promise is given that the "mountain of difficulty shall become a plain." Haggai is the prophet who, speaking again under divine inspiration, has urged the rulers and people to this enterprise, and in the name of God has promised them success. Emboldened by these assurances, we are willing to undertake new and even hazardous enterprises, and try to remove the rubbish of the Old prior to laying the foundation of the New.

As usual, earnest labor is rewarded by success, and every searcher discovers something that will be useful in the enterprise he has in hand. The element of the mysterious is still present, and in the deciphering of the mysteries memory and tradition are at fault, but the written "word of the Lord is precious in these days." To the Law and to the Testimony!

We open the book through which God of old spake to men, and there is the key that unravels the enigma and solves the problem and interprets the mystery. Raise, raise the Royal Arch! Place thereon the keystone of completion! In bated breath let each to the other, King to Scribe, and Scribe to Priest, and Priest to King again, Sojourner to Sojourner, and he to Sojourner again, repeat in syllables the sacred words, which in the three great nations of antiquity were used to designate the

Deity. The great mystery is solved! The toils of the pilgrims are accomplished. And in the supreme revelation of the sacred name of Deity we rest. God, the solution of every secret, God, the key that unlocks the phenomena of nature. God, the supreme trust and hope of humanity. God overarching all the firmaments, all the covenants, all the dispensations, and all the eternities!

"In the beginning God created the heavens and the earth." God "breathed into man's nostrils the breath of life, and man became a living soul." God "upholdeth all things by the word of His power." God continues immutable amidst time's immeasurable mutations. "Thou, Lord, in the beginning hast laid the foundation of the earth; and the heavens are the works of thine hands. They shall perish, but thou remainest; and they shall all wax old as doth a garment; and as a vesture shalt thou fold them up and they shall be changed; but thou art the same and thy years shall not fail."

The first Temple of the two Hirams and of Solomon shall decay. The second Temple of Joshua, Zerubbabel and Haggai shall crumble into dust. The third temple of Herod, wonder of the world, shall not have one stone left upon another by the invading Romans —

> "*And like the baseless fabric of a vision,*
> *All cloud-clapped towers, all gorgeous palaces, All solemn temples, the great globe itself,*
> *And all which it inherit, shall dissolve,*
> *And, like an insubstantial pageant faded, Leave not a rack behind.*"

But the Temple of the soul, the image of the Deity, shall survive the wreck of matter and the crash of worlds, and that Temple which the Lord doth build, a Temple not made with hands, shall be "eternal in the heavens." To the building of that human Temple; to the development and growth of character, we reconsecrate ourselves today. And, though human nature, like the first Temple, is in ruins, we determine in God's strength, and sustained by God's power and directed by God's wisdom, to rebuild this ruined human nature until it rises, complete and perfect, crowned with the capstone, held together by the keystone which the "builders rejected, but which is now the head stone of the corner," till the whole building, fitly framed and fashioned, is the abode of Deity world without end! Amen!

The Birth of Cryptic Masonry

By Hugh McCurdy

To Royal and Select Masters are given the keystone in Masonry, more precious than is known by the vast workers of the quarries; and it has been truthfully proclaimed that to preserve and transmit our principles to those who succeed us, in the hour of low twelve, is a sacred, bounden duty we owe to Cryptic Masonry. Thus believing, we should often revert to the origin of our Institution, for as has been said, it is only by digging to the foundation and examining each stone minutely that we can rightfully estimate what has been erected thereon. It is so with Freemasonry.

The first Grand Council which assembled at Jerusalem was composed of Solomon, King of Israel; Hiram, King of Tyre, and Hiram Abiff - the three Grand Masters, who, unobserved by "prying eyes," devised the entire plan by which the temple should be erected, how the workmen should be divided into various degrees, each class consisting of an independent body, whereby it might be recognized by the peculiar sign of that degree. Most happily, too, they combine within the power of the council the alpha and the omega of Freemasonry, thereby denominating Cryptic Masonry, by way of pre-eminence, the summit and perfection of Ancient Craft Masonry. Thus, in fact, the duties, the powers, the responsibilities of a council embrace the whole range of Ancient Craft Masonry, from the conception of the idea in the heart until the candidate is in the full possession of our mysteries, or in our own peculiar language, until he has passed the circle of perfection. It is in the secret vault, securely guarded, that the illustrious companions are required not only to search out the truth but to determine plans and design objects for the private as well as general good of the Craft.

If, therefore, companions who constitute this class and who have passed the circle of perfection - who have witnessed the wisdom, strength and beauty of our principles, would be but true to their obligations and faithful to their requirements, what immense good could be accomplished. No bickerings, no strife and no conflicts could ever exist in the Masonic institution, but peace, concord and tranquility would prevail, and the only contention in the whole Masonic family of earth would be who can best work and who can best agree. Brotherly love and charity would be happily blended together, and the life and character of a gentleman, of a faithful brother and devoted companion, would be merged in the life and purity of a consistent Mason. With you and all illustrious companions who have entered the secret vault rests the responsibility of confusion ever prevailing in the lodge, chapter or council. Hence you perceive that the charge of a Select Master is literally true when it says to each of, you "that your obligations are increased in proportion to your privileges; and also let it be your constant care to prove yourself worthy of the confidence reposed in you and of the high honor conferred on, you in admitting you among Select Masters."

The degrees of Entered Apprentice, Fellow Craft, and Master Mason were originally Ancient Craft Masonry; while the old constitutions gave the Master the right and authority to congregate his members into a chapter for the purpose of conferring the Royal Arch, which originally constituted a part of the Third degree. In elucidating the Royal Arch it becomes necessary that other degrees should be incorporated into the chapter for the purpose of explaining the various parts of the temple. Hence the Mark and Most Excellent Master's degrees were added and conferred before the Royal Arch.

In process of time it became necessary to establish a Council whose province it should be to "account for the concealment and preservation of those essentials of the Craft which were brought to light at the erection of the second temple, and which lay concealed from the mystic eye four hundred and seventy years." Hence Cryptic Masonry was inaugurated.

In different countries different systems prevail to inculcate, enforce and teach Ancient Craft Masonry; but in this country it is confined to the degrees of the lodge, chapter and council. Cryptic Masonry, therefore, is contained within the degrees of Royal and Select Masters, and are numbered eight and nine in the York rite, although in a chronological point of view they are the first and last degrees, hence called the alpha and omega of Ancient Craft Masonry. They illustrate the mysteries of Masonry, and without a full, perfect and complete knowledge of these degrees our Masonic edifice is incomplete and unfinished; or, as has been aptly said, "the degrees of Royal and Select Masters are polished and perfect ashlars, marked and numbered for the building."

Delos, an island of the Cyclades, was famed in ancient times for the number and skill of its artists, and for the splendid temple and oracle of Apollo, raised eventually as an asylum to his mother when she was pursued from place to place by the implacable Juno. From this famous oracle came the fount of inspiration, said to be a chasm from which issued the exhilarating vapor. Over this was built the tripod of the gods from which a populace could breathe the ascending distillations. To the Mason we need not enlarge this illustration. The soul grows as truly as the Mason grows - as the tree takes in the air of the universe, aided by dew and rain, and by its mysterious chemistry transmits sap and fiber into wood and leaf, and flower and fruit, and color and perfume, so does the soul of the Mason drink in living knowledge and by a divine alchemy, as patent and with the same inherent force as that which lies hid in the germ of the acorn. The virtuous Roman truly said, "Either let not that which seems expedient be base, or if it be base, let it not be expedient."

If our Masonic Order were merely a thing of yesterday; if it were local and confined to one country, or to men of one faith; or if the number of its initiates were limited to this or that clime, or its capacity for good or evil devoted to selfish ends, the question of its morality and philosophy might well be consigned to one grave. Not in vain are the winged seeds of truth ever sown. GOD sees that they take root somewhere and grow. The truth of all this is witnessed in the past history of nearly 6,000 years - their pungent facts have been figured on the breast-plate of time. When our ancient brethren dispensed their charities under the frowns of barbarism - when they disregarded the anathemas of kings and rulers and gathered around common altars in fraternal relations - they gave divine evidence that the Order would survive the mutations of time; and if we, brothers, shall continue to emulate the virtues of these good and faithful men, it will survive the wreck of ages yet to come.

Need I say more in honor of that Craft whose acts shine among the brightest in the domain of "good will to man?" Deeds of love, it may well be claimed, are the chief employment of the angels of GOD, and into a soul that overflows with bounty the bright-robed messengers of faith, hope and charity constantly descend. Our faith after death shall be swallowed up in victory; our hope consumed only by its enjoyment, and our charity ended when we shake off mortality in the boundless atmosphere of eternal love.

www.ingramcontent.com/pod-product-compliance
Lightning Source LLC
LaVergne TN
LVHW041457070426
835507LV00009B/654